Minute Motivators for Dieters

Stan Toler

BEACON HILL PRESS
OF KANSAS CITY

Copyright © 2002, 2011, 2014 by Stan Toler
Beacon Hill Press of Kansas City
PO Box 419527
Kansas City, MO 64141
www.BeaconHillBooks.com
ISBN 978-0-8341-3289-4
Printed in the
United States of America

Library of Congress Control Number: 2014941311

10 9 8 7 6 5 4 3 2 1

Introduction

Man does not live by celery alone!

Food alone doesn't make a diet. Right food choices are just one part of a successful diet plan. The other ingredients include direction, determination, and discernment. Dieting isn't just about what goes into your mouth. It's also about what goes into your mind.

Minute Motivators for Dieters will be your friend as you make wise decisions about your lifestyle, good choices about your future, and a careful evaluation of yourself.

Written with a "lite" touch, this book will enlarge your spirit as you reduce your calories.

Stan Toler

Dieting is a lifelong journey.

"Tough diets never last,

but tough dieters do."

—Mark Hollingsworth

CHOICES

A diet doesn't last for two weeks or two months. It isn't just about getting into that new dress or that new pair of pants for your twenty-fifth high school reunion. You know, the one where you'll meet those classmates you envisioned as being tiny as a twig— only to discover they've added a few "rings around the trunk" as well!

You're on a diet your whole life. Every bite you take is part of your daily diet—your necessary intake of food. So the diet you choose has to be one that will last—one that will keep you healthy for the long haul. Dieting is a series of daily choices that ultimately will be measured in how much you weigh and, in some cases, how long you live. What you decide about your dietary *options* today will directly affect your dietary *requirements* five, ten, or twenty years from now. In other words, brownies today, bulges tomorrow!

Don't try to cram a lifetime of good eating into one month. Choose eating habits that will last as long as you do.

Consult a doctor before you diet.

"My doctor has advised me
to give up those intimate little
dinners for four, unless, of course,
there are three other people
eating with me."

—Orson Welles

CAUTION

Don't jump on the fad-diet bandwagon. Man does not live by celery alone! Horror stories abound of fad dieters who have harmed their bodies—or lost their lives—by ignoring their need for a holistic approach to losing weight.

A little boy was asked what he would do when he got big like his daddy. He quickly replied, "Stop eating jelly donuts!" Common sense is just as important as carbohydrates. You don't have to give up reasoning just because you gave up coconut cream pie. Caution is in order. You've heard the expression, "Don't try this at home." It just may be that home isn't the best place to start a diet. Maybe it should be started at the doctor's office. Start with a professional opinion about weight loss, not the advice on page one of the inquiring-mind magazines at the grocery checkout counter.

Get the whole health view. Be sure that your body's need for nutrition will be met, even as you reduce your intake. In other words, proceed with caution.

Say No-No to Yo-Yo Dieting.

"No food tastes as good
as the food you eat when
you're cheating on a diet."

—Derl Keefer

STABILITY

If you have two sections in your closet marked "before" and "after," then maybe it's time to swear off yo-yo dieting. You know you can't live on turtle toenails forever! Up-and-down dieting is bad for your body, worse for your spirit. Avoid the temptation to shed a few pounds quickly on a diet that you can't sustain. Yo-yo dieting leads to frustration as you realize, "I always gain it right back." Easy off leads to easy on.

Take the long view; think months, not days. "I'm in this for the long 'overhaul.'" That late-night infomercial spokesperson with the simonized white teeth and the fifteen-inch waist may say she lost twenty pounds in two weeks, but she may not be talking about pounds. She might mean her basset hound ran away! Stability is key to successful dieting.

Adopt a plan that will meet your desire to be fit next year, not just your desire to look good next week. If you're going to hide the Gummi bears, then burn that map to their den!

To diet means to "do it!"

"A window of opportunity won't open itself."

—David M. Vaughn

RESOLVE

Dieting is a fifty-fifty proposition: 50 percent *will* and 50 percent *won't*. It's like deciding not to drive the wrong way on a one-way street. You make an on-the-spot decision based on the fear that your new pearl necklace won't fit around a neck brace.

Not only does dieting require an act of the "won't," it requires an act of the "will." Don't be fooled by fad diets that promise results without effort. To change your diet means to change your way of life. And that will take some resolve. You'll have to decide to change the way you think about food, about comfort, about yourself.

Saying no to food will be the easy part. Saying yes to new attitudes, new disciplines, new life habits— that's the hard part. It's a *New You* resolution, not a New Year's resolution.

Getting started is a "will" thing. But just like putting on a Speedo in the fitting room of the department store and deciding whether to look in the mirror, sooner or later, you'll have to "just do it!"

Establish a desired weight goal.

"Without a deadline, baby,

I wouldn't do nothing."

—Duke Ellington

GOALS

Dieting involves setting goals. Those goals will vary from individual to individual. Some set goals like losing enough weight so that when they tie their tennis shoes they don't need to have an oxygen tank handy. Others want to lose enough weight so that when they're driving a car, someone on the passenger side doesn't have to hold the seat belt.

Give yourself a target, and your diet is more likely to be successful. But dieting goals must be realistic. If everyone were a runway model, nobody would be left to applaud and take pictures. What is a reasonable weight for someone of your age, height, and body type? Is your goal reachable? Can you sustain that weight over the long term? What is your projected date to arrive at the goal? Find an appropriate goal and an appropriate time frame.

Setting a goal will give you something to work toward and a way to measure your success. And when you reach that goal, you won't have to wonder any longer whether or not your ankle socks are up!

Chart your progress.

"What you get by reaching
your goals is not nearly as
important as what you
become by reaching them."

—Zig Ziglar

EVALUATION

Milestones are important in dieting. Charting the number of days since you sat in a darkened closet and ate a whole carton of butter pecan ice cream is important. Evaluating your progress helps you take a look at where you've been and helps you to see where you're going.

Goals must be realistic, and goals must be measurable. It's not very flattering when someone tells you you've lost a "ton of weight," but it's a great incentive to know in your mind that you've lost eight pounds. Note your progress in specific terms. You know how exciting it is to put those tiny ruler marks on the wall to see how your little Johnny or Mary has grown. Try it on yourself. Now that doesn't mean putting erasable pen marks on the refrigerator and standing between them; it simply means keeping a record of your progress in weight loss. When you get discouraged, it'll help to see how far you've come.

Don't get rattled by daily ups and downs. Focus on the total picture, your overall weight-loss goal.

Take one step at a time.

"The giant oak is just an
acorn that held its ground."

—Mark Gilroy

PROGRESS

R ome wasn't built in a day. And weight loss doesn't happen overnight—unless you've donated your stomach to science while you're still living. Avoid the temptation to go for the "big drop." Easy off leads to easy on. Nobody runs the last laps of the race first. Champion runners understand the importance of every single stride in their race to the finish tape.

"Why did your family switch churches?" a woman asked her little nephew.

He answered, "Well, Dad likes a formal church."

"And what does he like about the formal church?" she continued.

The boy replied, "I dunno, I think he likes the lethargy."

Unlike liturgy (which is what the little boy really meant), lethargy is not a good thing. Dieting takes effort. You can't put a diet on autopilot and expect to steer around obstacles like chocolate éclairs.

Set some progress goals. Aim to lose a pound a week. Not only will you reach your goal, you'll also gain eating habits that will help you maintain your desired weight. You'll get there, one step at a time.

Enroll in a nutrition class.

"Everyone is health conscious these days. People who smoke, drink, overeat, never exercise— they're a dying breed."

—George Rice

SELECTION

A man on his third week of a starvation diet drove up to the window of the local fast-food restaurant. "May I take your order?" the voice on the intercom asked.

The dieter yelled in a panicky voice, "Yes, I'll have everything!"

The teenager at the other end of the intercom replied, "Uh, okay, would you like fries with that?"

There may be days when "everything" sounds a lot better than a "little of nothing." But eating "everything" is part of the problem. Selecting the right foods is key to dieting. You may not need to eat less food so much as you may need to eat *different* foods. Many people are overweight not because they eat too much, but because they eat the wrong things. Dieting isn't just about losing weight. It's also about feeding your body properly. Make it your business to learn about good nutrition. Find out which foods to eat more of, which to eat less of, and which to avoid entirely.

Don't just eat less. Eat right. You'll lose weight and gain energy.

Identify your obstacles.

"Lord, if You can't make me thin, then make my friends look fat."

—Erma Bombeck

PLANNING

An elderly lady went to a diet center and was met by a young attendant. "May I help you?"

"Yes," the lady responded, "I'm here to get one of those diets you talked about on TV."

"Madam," the attendant said, "you don't look like you need a diet. In fact, for your age you look rather fit."

Irritated at the young man's response, she replied, "Sonny, I'm here for a diet, and my age is nobody's business but mine!"

The young man answered sarcastically, "And it looks like you've been in business for a good while!"

Dieting is nobody's business but your own. You know yourself better than anyone else does. What are the things that will hinder your weight-loss effort? A favorite snack? Afternoon "munchies"? An unsupportive family member? Television time? Identifying your obstacles will be half the battle.

Then, determine what you will do about them. Change your daily routine. Enlist the help of friends. Steer clear of the vending machine.

Knowing what not to do is as important as knowing what to do.

Balance diet and exercise.

"My idea of a balanced diet is a quarter pounder in each hand."

—George Foreman

BALANCE

It was the husband's turn to fix dinner. "How about macaroni and cheese?" he inquired.

"Macaroni and cheese? You know that's fattening!" his wife answered. "How about bringing something to the table that will make me look slim and sexy."

So her husband sat an exercise bike by her chair.

Proper eating and proper exercise both have their place in dieting. And both can get out of control like a garden hose in the hands of a four-year-old. We eat in order to survive, yet we find pleasure in eating. We exercise because it's good for us, but exercise is also a great stress reliever. Calories aren't burned on the stove; they're burned on the exercise bike or the treadmill.

A proper balance of diet and exercise will go a long way in helping you reach your diet goals. Try not to eat because it feels good or because certain foods bring comfort. Balance diet and exercise programs. Strike the balance between painful self-denial and unhealthy over-indulgence.

Enjoy exercise, but don't exercise to excess. Enjoy eating, but don't live to eat.

Drop out of the "clean-plate club."

"Lord, help me to eat more
heartily at Your table and
more sparingly at mine!"

—Derl Keefer

MODERATION

An outspoken grandma looked around the American Legion hall filled with wedding guests and grabbed the groom by the arm, "Most of these folks your family?"

"Why, yes, they are," the startled groom replied, "Why do you ask?"

She answered, "Wondering how many kids you're thinkin' about havin', 'cause from the looks of this place, self-control obviously doesn't run in the family!"

Self-control doesn't run in anyone's family. It's a learned habit. For example, from early childhood you have been admonished to clean your plate, a clean plate often leading to a reward. Advertisers beckon eaters to indulge their every craving. And, in some instances, they claim that the indulgence will enhance your quality of life. "Eat it for your health." They're inviting you to join the "clean-plate club."

But overindulgence will seldom enhance the quality of life. In fact, the reverse is true. Learn the secret of moderation. Learn to eat only what your body needs, which may be different from what's on the table — or on your plate.

Get out of
the house.

"Home is where the

heartburn is."

—Charlie Haddock

CHANGE

Effective dieting isn't about weight loss so much as life change. No diet will be successful if it's not accompanied by changes in behavior that will support good eating habits. Home is the place to start. "Home is where the heart is." That's a warm fuzzy saying. Home is also where the potato chips are. Home is where the cookies are stored on the top shelf of the food pantry by the refrigerator. Sometimes a change of scenery will help relieve the "munchies" in your mind.

And that change of scenery is not just food related. A different environment is good for the soul as well as the body. Having just moved from Arizona to Pennsylvania, a new little resident saw her first snow, "Momma! Come out here quick! God dumped popcorn all over our yard last night!"

Maybe it's time for you to get out of the house and see some "popcorn" for yourself. Add activity to your life. Find new interests or expand old ones. If you're locked into a self-defeating routine, look for some loose *change*.

Overcome a sedentary lifestyle with activity.

"If you ever see me jogging—

you'll know the laxative

is working."

—Rodney Dangerfield

ACTIVITY

C ontrary to popular opinion, most people can chew gum and walk at the same time! The problem is that most of us aren't trying it. We're passive people. On the whole we live stationary, sedentary lives. For some, their idea of exercise is picking up the remote control after it drops off the arm of their La-Z-Boy. It's a way of life that is taking its toll on our society. We sit more than we stand, and we ride more than we walk.

It takes effort to inject activity into your daily routines. But activity is exactly what the dieter needs. You don't necessarily need a ten-speed treadmill with a water-mist sprayer and high-definition television attached to the handlebars to overcome a sedentary lifestyle. Look for opportunities to double-time—to combine exercise with a normally sedentary activity. Exercise while you watch the news. Jog while you pray. Walk while you're on the phone.

There are hundreds of add-on activities that can help you overcome the sedentary life. Try some.

Recognize
your own self-worth.

"Self-worth is more important

than net worth."

—Talmadge Johnson

SELF-ESTEEM

If the saying is true, "You are what you eat," then many folks think they're junk. Good dieting begins with a good attitude. Junk food and junky attitudes usually go hand in hand. Your attitude about yourself will be the key to success in your diet—or anything else. Recognize that you are a person of worth.

You're not like the man in the classic story who came home from a visit to the psychiatrist and reported to his wife, "The doctor says I have an inferiority complex."

She replied quickly, "That's not true!"

"That's what I thought," the man responded.

His wife added, "It's no complex; you really are inferior!"

Your Creator doesn't agree. The Scripture says he looked on all of his creation and declared it a winner. That doesn't excuse bad behavior or unwise choices, but it does say something about natural resources.

When you begin to think positively about yourself, you will begin to treat yourself differently. Your own self-image is the most important weapon in your battle for good health.

Exercise your mind.

"If you want to learn something
new, don't act like you
already know it."

—James M. Carter

INTELLECT

The six-year-old son of an Ivy League college professor came sulking through the back door dragging his backpack. Seeing his forlorn look, his mother inquired, "Son, you look a little discouraged. What seems to be the matter?"

"Mom, I'm tired of the same old thing: Get up, go to school, come home, study, go to bed, get up, go to school. If it's all right with you, next year I'm taking a sabbatical."

Philosophers may argue the distinction between body, mind, and spirit, but for the dieter there is none. What you think directly affects what you do and how you feel. If your body is out of shape, it's likely that your mind is too.

Don't take a sabbatical from learning. Cultivate the intellect. Dust off your brain and put to work. Read a book. Take a class. Borrow some learning tapes. Volunteer to be a teacher's aide. Put your mind on an exercise program. Open it to new horizons. An open mind is like an open window: it lets in the sunshine.

Quit making excuses.

"You can't escape the

responsibility of tomorrow

by evading it today."

—Abraham Lincoln

RESPONSIBILITY

The first step to climbing out of the bed of lethargy is to throw off the covers. "I can't." "It's too difficult." "It'll take too long." "I'll never make it." Nonsense! There aren't many innocent victims in the weight war. With few exceptions, we are what we have decided to eat.

The Sunday School teacher was explaining the story of Moses and the Ten Commandments. When he got to the part about the tablets of stone, the junior high boy in the back of the class interrupted, "Tablets of stone? What do you swallow *those* tablets with? Mineral water?"

The Ten Commandments aren't that hard to swallow! They were given to us as a yardstick of moral behavior. In addition to giving them to us, God gave us a choice as to whether or not to obey them. We all are responsible for the choices we make. For example, no one can force you to eat well or to eat poorly. You make the choices that determine the blessing or bane of eating. Take responsibility for yourself and your actions.

Just say "NO!"

"It is better to be slow-tempered
than famous; it is better to
have self-control than to
control an army."

—Proverbs 16:32

SELF-CONTROL

Trying to lose weight without using any self-control is like trying to ride a bicycle without handlebars. You may get on down the road a bit, but soon there's going to be a crash. Dieting schemes abound that promise dramatic results with no effort. "Take these pills, and you'll lose pounds while you sleep," the late-night television commercial claims. But the only thing you lose is the nineteen dollars and ninety-eight cents, plus shipping and handling, which you charged to your credit card! You will never be in control of your weight or your health—or any other area of your life—until you learn to control yourself. That begins by learning to say "No!"

Self-control begins in the mind. You make some mental choices. Option A or Option B. Which has long-term spiritual, physical, social, or financial benefits? Then, you put up some "fences" for your own safety. You keep certain foods or certain behaviors out of your life—for your own protection.

If you want to lose weight, be "in the 'No!'"

Sip some soup.

"Variety's the very spice of life
that gives it all its flavor."

—William Cowper

VARIETY

Two construction workers sat on a steel beam high above the ground. One of the workers popped open his lunch box and pulled out a Cheez Whiz sandwich. His co-worker commented, "Cheez Whiz sandwiches? Wasn't that same thing in your lunch box yesterday?"

"You got that right!" the worker answered.

"Well, if I were you, I'd tell that cook to add a little variety to the menu," the coworker added.

"Tell him yourself," the worker responded. "I packed those sandwiches!"

What's for lunch? You'll probably name the two or three favorite foods that you eat nearly every day. Maybe it's time to give up Cheez Whiz sandwiches. Variety is a good alternative for the dietary ho-hums. If your body is stuck in a rut, that's only because your mind is. Add some variety to your diet. Think beyond the obvious choices. Sip some soup for a change.

When you can answer the question, "What's for lunch?" with something besides "a burger and fries," you'll be a couple of steps closer to your weight-loss goals.

Drink a
diet cola.

Diet cola: "a drink you buy at
the convenience store to go
with a candy bar."

—Earl Blair Jr.

ALTERNATIVES

Are you still counting those calories?" the neighbor asked as she watched her friend dip the last remnants of ice cream from the bottom of the soda glass.

"Yes," her friend replied, "but I think I just lost count!"

The carbonated-drink advertisement used to say, "It's the real thing." And they were right: real sugar, real calories, and real pounds. Maybe the real isn't really that good for you. "You are what you eat," the axiom claims. If so, then "you are what you drink" as well. Dietary choices cover all areas of our daily intake.

Successful dieters don't give up everything. They just give up the wrong things. You can satisfy your taste for many foods by substituting healthier alternatives. The same company that offers a sugar-packed soda also offers a sugar-free soda. Ask yourself, *Am I more concerned with the taste of a beverage or its effect on my body?* The choices get easier after that. Make the switch to diet drinks. Who knows, you might even be drinking good old water in no time.

Listen to your body and quit eating when you are full.

"When it comes to eating, you can
help yourself more by
helping yourself less."

—Jenny Craig

SATISFACTION

W hy do you eat? There's no doubt that eating is a pleasure, but eating for pleasure is a problem.

"That's the third helping of potatoes," a concerned wife whispered to her husband at a restaurant meeting with friends. "What does that tell you?"

Her husband replied, "The meat loaf isn't that great?"

If you listen to your body, you'll hear more than commentaries on the meat loaf. Often it says, "I'm full; give me a break!" Your body is your best dietary consultant. Why spend hundreds of dollars getting dieting advice from an outsider when your have a custom-made, onboard dietary indicator. Listen when it tells you that you are stuffing rather than satisfying.

You can pour only so much coffee into a cup. Beyond that, it's a disaster in the making. Be thankful that you have enough to eat. Eat your fill, but don't overfill. Continuing to eat when your stomach is filled will result in more than discomfort—it will perpetuate the deeper problem of eating for the wrong reasons.

Never eat in the car.

"If carrots are so good for my eyes,

how come I see so many dead

rabbits on the highways?"

—Richard Jeni

FOCUS

The modern car has become much more than a mode of transportation. Now it's a phone booth, beauty shop, television room, camper, and classroom. It also serves as a mobile dining room. Thanks to drive-thru windows and take-out foods, you can easily meet or exceed your calorie quota in the middle of a traffic gridlock. But eating in the car might give you more than motion sickness; it could give you motion *thickness*.

Did you know that the car is one of the places where it's easiest to overeat? It seems that driving and munching go hand in hand. It's far too easy to keep one hand on the wheel and the other in a bag of chips. And whether they're grilled, fried, blackened, baked, or skewered, fast foods are generally not very diet-friendly.

Maintain your focus. Don't allow eating to become an add-on to other activities—especially driving. Not only will you keep yourself from some calories, you might keep from colliding with that driver in the other lane!

Don't mix alcohol with dieting.

"Stop and think before

you drink."

—Howard Hunt

TEMPERANCE

O ne old boy who had a problem with alcohol donated his liver to science. A few weeks after his demise, his widow received a letter from the medical institution. "Dear Madam, we're returning your husband's liver. We appreciate the thought, but we're not that desperate!"

There are many reasons why alcohol and dieting aren't a good mix. Never mind that many alcoholic beverages are high in calories. Alcohol is a detriment to your dieting initiative because it attacks your center of control: your mind. The battle you face in losing weight is more about mind-control than body-control. Self-control, discipline, self-denial, and per-severance— these are your weapons in the war on weight. You have made a decision to add discipline to your eating routine. Alcohol always hurts the pursuit of discipline.

Actually, alcohol isn't a good mix with anything. But it's especially a bad mix with dieting. Temperance and discipline are natural allies. Saying "No!" to alcohol will make it easier to exercise self-control in other areas—like fettuccine Alfredo for instance.

Go easy on the sugar.

"Do you like honey?
Don't eat too much of it,
or it will make you sick!"

—Proverbs 25:16

RESTRAINT

A stand-up comedian once commented that he used so much artificial sweetener, he had become artificially sweet. Almost any food is healthy if eaten in proper portions. And almost any food can be dangerous when overconsumed.

Learn that there's a place for every food, and learn to keep every food in its place. One of the first ingredients to get control over is sugar. At times it seems that sugar is the soil of the earth. Candy stores and bakeries build their businesses on the foundation of that granulated gladness. They may hide it in their storefront delicacies, but one bite and you know you've found it!

You don't have to be a sugar slave. Take control. Start by putting your sugar intake within proper limits. Identify the sources of sugar in your diet. How many of them should be reduced or eliminated? Sugared cereals, soft drinks, candy, desserts—all of them are okay, in the proper proportions. But if you *don't* keep them in their proper proportions, you won't be in yours.

Reduce the fat intake.

"You know your fat intake
is too much if the finger
prick for your cholesterol
screening yields gravy."

—Jerry Brecheisen

MODERATION

Proper dieting includes exercise. And when it comes to eating fatty foods, one of the best exercises is turning your head, first to the left and then to the right. That not only will help your neck muscles, it will be of great benefit to your stomach muscles as well.

At times, self-restraint is just as important as self-denial. Saying "No" all the time—to every food—leads to diet failure. Reward yourself with a diet day off. If you reach a diet goal, give yourself half of that aluminum-wrapped brownie you've been hiding in the desk drawer!

Remember the advertisement, "I can't believe I ate the whole thing!" Don't follow that lead. Eat a portion—enough to keep your inspiration alive but not enough to put the wrecking ball to your diet house. Moderation means pulling in the reins from time to time, keeping yourself in check. It means limiting portion sizes. It means choosing the lesser of two dietary evils.

By keeping fat in its place, you'll keep fat from those other places!

Remember:
The fat is in your head!

"Our life is what our

thoughts make it."

—Marcus Aurelius

ATTITUDE

A lady went to her doctor for a follow-up appointment. "Doc, the diet just isn't working," she reported.

The doctor asked, "Did you follow the diet plan I gave you?"

"No, I just couldn't stick to it," she answered.

"Did you exercise like I told you?" the doctor continued.

She replied, "No, it was just too hard."

The doctor responded, "Then I have one last word of advice."

"What's that?" the lady asked.

"You'd better memorize how your feet look!"

You can't change your weight until you change your thinking—until you're convinced that you *can* change your behavior, that you can look and feel different. Don't fall for defeatist deceptions: "It's no use." "I'll be this way forever."

Open your mind. Visualize yourself in that new suit or dress. Picture yourself on that South Sea island beach in that new swimming suit.

Change your attitude. Think positively about yourself. Appreciate your good qualities. Believe that you can. Say, "I *can* learn to eat differently. I can do this!"

Believe me, you can!

Think: "I'm looking better every day."

"Whether you think you can

or you think you can't,

you are right."

—Loraine Teaberry

SELF-IMAGE

Two dieters were eating their salads with low-calorie dressing, Melba toast, and celery sticks. "You know, Doris," one of the dieters suddenly spoke up, "my doctor said this diet would add years to my life. He was right about that! I started this stupid diet three weeks ago on my fortieth birthday, and already I feel like a skinny old woman!"

It's true. Beauty really is in the eye of the beholder. Your image of yourself will affect your health and your behavior. If you see yourself as unattractive and worthless, you'll behave accordingly. When you begin to see yourself as worthwhile, attractive, and changing for the better, you'll begin to make healthier choices.

Give yourself a pep talk. Compliment yourself on reaching your goal. "I'm making great progress!" "I'm looking better all the time!" Recognize your good qualities. "I really am an attractive person!"

When you acknowledge your qualities, and when you give yourself credit for your achievements, you'll begin to see yourself in a bright new light. And you'll see others seeing you in that same light.

Control your diet.

"I am not a vegetarian because

I love animals; I am

a vegetarian because

I hate plants."

—A. Whitney Brown

INDEPENDENCE

One mark of maturity is the realization that you aren't dependent on others to make your dietary choices. Mature people make those choices for themselves. Former president George Bush angered the vegetable growers but declared his independence when he said that he was an adult and no one was going to make him eat broccoli anymore.

Broccoli may be one of your favorites. But maybe you've been pressured into eating other foods—some high in calories and low in nourishment—just to please the lunch crowd. It's time to declare your independence by choosing to eat foods that will help you reach your diet goals, not foods that will just help you feel like you're one of the gang.

Don't allow your host, the waiter, or your friends to determine how much you will eat or what you will eat. Make that decision for yourself. Determine what menu items are best for you, and stick with *your* choice.

You're an adult now. You don't have to eat broccoli, or any other food, if you don't want to.

Remember:
God is your source.

"When we do what we can,

God will do what we can't."

—Terry N. Toler

FAITH

The children's church teacher finished her Bible story about Daniel in the lions' den. "Children, can anyone tell me why those mean old lions didn't have Daniel for breakfast?" she asked.

A little girl on the front row waved her hand wildly. "I know! I know!"

The teacher pointed to her and said, "Then tell the class."

Proudly, the little girl answered, "Because they would have choked on his backbone!"

Faith in God builds healthy backbones. Food can give strength to your body, but never to your soul. Abandon the notion that food can bring you comfort or security. No thing can do that. Only God can. Don't look to anything, or *anyone*, to give you peace, comfort, or strength, other than Him.

Recognize God as your source of strength. A healthy diet includes spiritual disciplines such as daily prayer and Bible reading, as well as physical disciplines. You'll find that when you experience wholeness in the inner person, it will be reflected in every other area of your life.

Never Forget: Losing weight is a matter of mind over platter.

"As a child, my family's
menu consisted of two
choices; take it, or leave it."

—Buddy Hackett

OUTLOOK

A preacher was having dinner with his wife after what he perceived to be one of his greatest Sunday sermons. With a swaggering attitude, he asked, "Darlin', just how many awesome preachers do you think you've listened to over the years?"

Reading his mind, as usual, his wife responded, "Oh, I don't know. I've heard many great preachers. But I have an idea the list is a little bit shorter than what you might be thinking about right now!"

You really are what you think you are. Positive attitudes result in positive actions. One key to a successful diet is a positive outlook. In the battle between you and the food, you *will* win. You must first believe that you can achieve your goal.

Adopt a positive attitude toward your diet and your health. Believe that you can change your mind, your body, and your life. Don't allow yourself to be controlled by external forces. Take control of your attitude. Take control of your life. Believe that you can succeed.

You can lose weight!

Never use food binges as a reward.

Overeating—

"The destiny that shapes our ends."

—Jackie Gleason

PURPOSE

One country song has the interesting lyric, "Momma, bring a hammer. There's a fly on Poppa's head." A hammer is an excellent tool. But it makes a lousy flyswatter. Food is intended to sustain our strength while bringing modest pleasure, but it is not intended to be the icing on the cake of life.

Some folks celebrate their dieting efforts with a food binge. But overindulgence is a poor reward system. Avoid the temptation to reward yourself by "breaking all the rules." Food misdemeanors can quickly turn into food felonies. It's one thing to go out for a nonfat yogurt to celebrate the loss of a pound or two. It's another thing to take a shovel along!

Eating right is not boring. Eating properly should be pleasurable. Developing a taste for foods that are good for you takes discipline and time. But diving into foods that simply taste good to you takes little effort and results in disastrous effects.

Overeating should never be a reward for exercising discipline in another area of your life.

Avoid the elevator— try the stairs!

"I'll bicycle, ski,
and dance for hours.
I'll do all the sports that
require hot showers.
I love to play golf,
and miss most my putts,
But taking the stairs
just drives me nuts!"

—Anonymous

ACTIVITY

A passive lifestyle is just as dangerous as a large appetite. The only activity some folks get is jumping to conclusions and spreading rumors. What you do (or don't do) affects your health just as much as what you eat does. Many people are sedentary. They drive to work and sit at a desk all day. Then they come home and relax on the couch! For the next several hours, they sit or recline in a semiconscious state through a barrage of mindless television shows.

Alter your lifestyle. Inject some exercise into your routine. Look for ways to stay active throughout the day. Take the stairs instead of the elevator. Take a walk at lunchtime. Park your car at the far end of the parking lot instead of the VIP space next to the office building. Do some desk-side exercises. Walk a treadmill or pedal an exercise bike during daytime television viewing. Or, turn off the television and go outdoors for some yard work, exercise, or good ol' visiting with your neighbors at the fence.

Try to avoid buffet meals.

"Long meals make short lives."

—Sir John Lubbock

EXCESS

All you can eat." Those four little words spell success for some restaurants, but they spell danger for many dieters. Buffet-style restaurants and dinner parties are dietary hazards because they encourage us to eat in excess. Some restaurants have changed their signs to read "All you *care* to eat." But the only care some diners exhibit is an "I don't care" attitude.

A marksman famous for shooting BB guns was interviewed on a local, noontime news show. "I understand that you hit the bull's-eye almost 100 percent of the time. That must take a lot of practice," the television host commented.

The marksman said, "That and the help of my lovely assistant, Marabell." The camera panned over to the assistant sitting on the far end of the couch. Her face was noticeably pockmarked; she had bandages on her forehead; and her eyeglasses were shattered until only the rims were intact. "You see," the shooter continued, "the moment I shoot, Marabell adjusts the target."

Don't move the target. Select a restaurant that serves sensible portions, and learn to say "When."

Lose weight
with a friend.

"Friends are God's

life preservers."

—Doug Carter

PARTNERSHIP

True friends will stay with you in "thickness and in health." But that friend may be just exactly what you need to help you reach your diet goals. People really do need each other. That's the way we're made. Most projects are made easier when you have a coworker.

Try "team dieting." Find a friend who also wants to shed a few pounds. Meet together over coffee (no sugar) and two low-fat cookies to map out your strategy. Set some common food boundaries. Project some reasonable weight-loss goals. Make a promise to encourage each other with comments, telephone calls, notes, and e-mail. And most of all, hold each other accountable: "How did you do today?" "How's your attitude?" "Did you walk past the vending machine?" "Did you succumb to the pizza buffet?" Having to face tough questions will help you stay on target.

And the benefits are mutual. Your encouragement may be just what your teammate needs to reach his or her diet goals.

"Here's to *our* health!"

Fill up on crunchy vegetables.

"Nothing stretches slacks
like snacks."

—Chuck Crow

CHOICE

J ust because you're trying to lose weight doesn't mean you have to go hungry all the time. There are foods that will satisfy your desire to eat without destroying your diet. It's a matter of making the right choices. For instance, how many rabbits have you seen at a weight-loss center? They've decided to fill up on such healthy foods as carrots, celery, and lettuce!

Nachos, potato chips, candy bars—we love these foods because they're so satisfying to eat. They crunch when you bite into them, and they make you feel full. But try some broccoli or cauliflower dipped in a low-fat dressing. Over time, substitutes will become the main thing.

You don't have to scale that mile-high chocolate cake at your favorite restaurant. Scaling a mile-high cake and scaling a mountain both have one thing in common: In either case, you'll soon need oxygen!

You can still eat. Just choose to eat right. Eat a lot of "little," and soon you'll be more little than lot!

Don't weigh
every day.

"The only thing that gives
you more for your money
today than it did a year ago
is a weighing machine."

—Jerry Brecheisen

PACE

A man visited his cardiologist after having a pacemaker put in. The doctor began to ask how he was adjusting to the new apparatus. The man responded, "It's great. I feel a lot better. The only difference I noticed was that tiny clicking sound."

"Does the noise bother you?" the doctor asked.

The man answered, "No, sir. But I bet the silence would!"

Dieters need to set a pace. You're in this for life, not just for a while. Don't become obsessed with your daily weight. You'll become too excited by small improvements and too devastated by minor setbacks.

Get on the scales once or twice a week if you have to. But don't set up camp there. Weigh only to keep yourself on track. That way, it'll keep you from losing focus. Remember the tortoise and the hare? The hare was faster but didn't make the impact that the tortoise did. Slower really is better when it comes to losing weight. Pick up the pace, and, more than likely, you'll pick up the pounds.

Never eat until you're hungry.

"You cannot reason with a hungry

belly; it has no ears."

—Greek Proverb

TIMING

You've heard the story of the lady who said she ate according to the rays of the sun. "When it's light, I start eating!" We're programmed to eat certain things at certain times. Why? It seems that we eat more from habit than necessity. Break the habit. Your body will tell you when it needs food just like an automobile will tell you when it needs fuel. Listen to it.

Just because the short hand is on one number and the long hand is on another, don't think you have to have a heavy meal. The clock, or anything else, shouldn't rule your diet. You should be in charge. Your body will call you to supper. Your Creator put a foolproof system in "at the factory."

And don't store up food like a squirrel, thinking, *I'll be hungry later*. Eat when you're hungry, not before. Eat enough to satisfy your body's needs, and no more. More than likely, there'll be some food left in the spring.

Drink water before eating a meal.

"Water, taken in moderation,

cannot hurt anybody."

—Mark Twain

STRATEGY

A little boy sat with his mother on the front row of the church. The preacher was really waxing eloquent. Pacing like a tiger at the zoo, he punctuated his sermon with pointing fingers and waving arms. Suddenly he stopped and reached under the pulpit for a glass of water. One sip and he began preaching again, with even more enthusiasm. The little boy elbowed his mother and cupped his hand over his mouth as he whispered into her ear, "It's just like a paddle-wheel boat! The water's driving him on!"

Water is a driving force in your diet program. There's no trick to this. When your stomach is full, you don't feel like eating anymore. If your stomach is half full to begin with, you'll eat less. Increasing your fluid intake has many health benefits; curbing your appetite is one of them. Start the habit of drinking water before and during your meals. You'll be surprised at how a few ounces of liquid help to extinguish the "hungrys."

Focus on the positive.

"The optimist has no brakes;

the pessimist has no motor."

—Melvin M. Maxwell

DISCOURAGEMENT

L osing weight is a struggle. Maintaining good dietary habits doesn't come naturally to most people. You can expect to become discouraged from time to time. Don't stay there. Don't look at where you are. Look at where you're going.

A little girl fell out of her bed with a thud. Her mother went running into her room, "What in the world happened? I heard you all the way downstairs."

Dusting herself off and straightening her pajamas, the little girl responded, "Well, Mother, I guess I was moving around in my bed, and I just got too close to where I got in!"

Don't be dominated by a setback. There will be times when you lose a battle or skirmish here and there. But that doesn't mean you've lost the war. Dieting should always be in the future tense, not the past tense. Dwell on where you are going, not on where you are or where you have been. The direction in which you choose to look will determine the course of your progress.

Remember:
Calories do count!

"Never eat more than

you can lift."

—Miss Piggy

DETAILS

You may think you're counting calories, but the fact of the matter is, calories are counting too. For example, while you're adding them, they're multiplying you!

Putting a collar on calories is essential to effective weight loss. Try this. Take a pencil and paper and write down everything you eat during the day. Now figure the number of calories for each item you've consumed. Add them up. The total will astound you.

Two mountain climbers reached the summit after a record-setting climb. Their months of planning and training had finally paid off. One of the climbers shouted, "We made it! Quick, Fred, get that video camera!"

Suddenly Fred looked despondent, "Uh, I thought you were bringing the camera."

Details really are important, especially in your menu selection. Some foods are more calorie-rich than others. It's possible that you can greatly reduce your *calorie* intake without greatly reducing your *volume* intake. In other words, you may be able to get less bang per bite if you'll count the calories.

Order the turkey instead of the T-bone.

"Diets are mainly food for thought."

—N. Wylie Jones

CHANGE

From fast-food hamburgers to fine-dining prime rib, we love our red meat. That little old lady in the classic television commercial asked, "Where's the beef?" We know the answer. It's all over our daily menus. A little dietary change may be just the ticket for the "weight-loss express." Try some white meat in your diet.

Two brothers were choosing from the kiddie menu at a restaurant. Each item had a picture by it to make it easier for the children to order. One of the items had a clown face by it. Their mom suggested, "Boys, why don't you order the 'Clown.'"

One of the brothers turned to the other and whispered, "Okay, but I bet it'll taste funny."

Try something new. Grilled sandwiches, subs, tacos, Chinese food—all of these can be prepared with turkey instead of beef. You may not have to give up your favorite food; just prepare it differently. It may take some adjustment, but the change of pace will eventually pay off at the scales.

Get out of the fast-food rut.

"You can find your way across the country using burger joints the way a navigator uses stars."

—Charles Kuralt

SELECTION

You've heard the expression "as American as apple pie." Not anymore! Apple pie has a challenger. Now we may say "as American as a double cheeseburger and a large order of fries." There's nothing wrong with a sandwich and a side order now and then, but there's more to life than scorched meat and greased potato scrapings. Sample some foods that are lower in fat. Jared, a college student with a weight problem, lost 235 pounds and gained national recognition by switching to Subway sandwiches and adding exercise to his daily routine.

A third-grader visited a museum of modern art with his father. As they stood in front of a painting that was a purple canvas with one red spot in the center, the boy commented on the emptiness of the canvas: "Look, Dad! Somebody stole the rest of the painting!"

If your diet is limited to certain fast foods, you might be missing out on the rest of the diet picture. Get out of the fast-food rut. Try a sandwich that's lower in fat. You might even try Jared's diet.

Try fasting and prayer.

"Life's road is rough, but you
can make it; hold out your hand,
and God will take it."

—Lon Woodrum

SPIRITUALITY

A middle-aged man looked at the locker-room mirror and commented to his gym partner, "George, ya' gotta admit it; the muscles are still there." His buddy responded, "Yep, they're still there. They just don't live in the same neighborhood!"

Your body is only part of your self. You may spend time each day exercising it and neglect the only thing about you that will last forever: your soul. Get your spirit in shape as well as your flesh. It takes discipline to exercise every day. But you know from experience that exercise is important to your diet. Spiritual exercise is also important.

Try fasting. A "fast" means to deny yourself something, such as a meal, for the purpose of spending that time in prayer. Don't use fasting as your primary dieting strategy, but recognize its value for your total health. The discipline of going without food will spill over into other areas of your life. Your waistline will diminish, but your spirit will be enriched.

Be careful with the caffeine.

"I've been on a diet for
two weeks, and all I've
lost is two weeks."

—Totie Fields

DISCERNMENT

The doctor asked his patient about her diet, "Do you drink a lot of water?"

"Not much," she replied. "I drink quite a bit of coffee though."

"More than three cups a day?" the concerned doctor inquired.

She answered, "Three cups? Why, I spill that much on the kitchen table every day!"

Discernment is vital to the diet process. Only you can make the food choices that will positively affect your diet. You know that some foods may indirectly deter your weight-loss efforts. You don't need a "doctor in the house" to know which foods are detrimental to your health and which are beneficial. Set up your own quality control. Look beyond the fat content and learn to evaluate the effect of what you consume on your total health.

Like any drug, caffeine has its side effects. As a stimulant, it's also known to fuel the appetite. The coffee, tea, or soft drink that you enjoy may be low in calories but may affect your body in undesirable ways. Think before you drink.

Write out your
life mission.

"Make long-range plans as
if you are going to live forever,
and live today as if it were
your last day on earth."

—Orville Hagan

PURPOSE

J ack!" the driver's education teacher shouted as her pupil turned the wrong way on a one-way street. "Do you know where you're going?"

Unfazed, the young driver responded, "No, Ma'am, but it looks like we're the only ones headin' in this direction."

What's your direction? What are you doing with your life? I don't mean right now. I'm talking about the big picture. What are your long-term plans? What is your life about? Why are you here? When you find solid answers to those questions, you'll discover new discipline for all areas of life.

You may have outlined your diet plan. The menu may be in order, but how about the rest of your life? Where do you want to be in five years? Ten years? Get alone with your Bible, your notebook, and your journal. Reflect on where you've been, where you are now, and where you want to be in your life journey.

When your life has purpose, your physical health is much easier to manage. Begin by pondering this question: What is my mission in life?

Establish your personal values.

"The world has forgotten, in its concern with left and right, that there is an above and below."

—Glen Drake

STANDARDS

W hat floor?" the polite young elevator operator asked.

"Thirteen, please," an elegantly dressed lady answered.

"Do you have business on that floor?" the operator asked.

"Really! What makes you think that's any of your business, young man?" the rider snapped.

Keeping his eye on the rising numbers and his finger on the controls, the young man quietly responded, "Because there are only twelve floors in this building, Ma'am."

Do you believe in telling the truth? What matters to you? What are your values? Is self-discipline important to you? What about integrity, morality, and faith? A mission statement deals with what you are doing. Personal values determine *how* you will do it.

Do you have lines you refuse to cross? Where does that determination come from? Your character will affect every area of your life—from your diet to your dating. Think about your personal values. Do you want to be thinner, look younger, or be physically fit because of some selfish motive? Or do your life goals come from an inner strength? Character counts—even more than calories.

Lighten up.

"Life is serious, but it
can't be taken seriously."

—Mark Hollingsworth

HUMOR

How's the diet going?" one man said to his friend.

"Well, it's going! I enrolled in a Yoga class to help it out."

His friend responded, "You're really practicing Yoga? I can't believe it!"

"It works great!" the dieter replied. "It didn't help me lose much weight, but I can eat in some pretty interesting positions!"

Don't take yourself so seriously! Certainly you want to lose weight, stay fit, and be healthy. All of that takes some attention, but life is for living, not analyzing! The "light" shouldn't be limited to your cream cheese. Put a little light in the rest of your life as well. Lighten up! Learn to laugh. Tell a joke. Look on the humorous side. There's a lot of sun behind those gray skies. There's a "partly sunny" in every situation. Look for it with a twinkle in your eye.

Don't think about yourself all the time. Look for a jolly, new friend. Share a few good stories. Spend time listening, rather than talking about yourself. Relax and learn to enjoy life!

Eat like a king for breakfast, like a prince for lunch, and like a pauper for dinner.

"Eat all you want . . .

just don't swallow."

—Tony Douglas

TIMING

According to my Grandma Brewster, we eat backwards. She meant that, in terms of the volume of food, we take our meals in the wrong order. In the morning, when our bodies are crying for fuel, we generally eat the smallest meal of the day. A piece of burned toast, an instant breakfast drink, and we're out the door to face our daily quota of giants. It's no wonder we feel weaker than a flea with the flu at mid-morning. We haven't given ourselves the food advantage.

Dinner can be a problem time as well. In the evening, when we're facing the day's longest period of inactivity, we usually eat the largest meal. We stop at our favorite restaurant and order without giving much thought to the length of time we'll be wearing that meal. And soon we're plopped down in that leather lounge chair with a remote in one hand and, in the other, the Styrofoam-boxed cheesecake the waiter saved for us. Reverse that. Eat a heartier breakfast and a lighter lunch. Eat the least in the evening.

Eat half as much and twice as often.

"Hey diddle diddle

I've a bulge in my middle

And hope to whittle it soon,

But eating's such fun

That I won't get it done

'Til my dish runs away

with my spoon!"

—The Royal Neighbor

FREQUENCY

If dietary discipline is a problem, six small meals would be better than three lingering trips around the buffet table. You know that your auto's carburetor controls the flow of fuel to the engine. Too much fuel at one time will stall the engine and leave you stranded in front of that nice man with the red face and bulging eyes you see in your rearview mirror. The carburetor knows that a little fuel at the right time is better than a lot of fuel all at once.

Good nutrition is delivering the right amounts of food fuel to your body. The "when" and the "how" of eating are just as important as the "why" and "where." It's been suggested that eating smaller meals more frequently is better than consuming large amounts two or three times a day. In other words, don't overfill your gas tank.

Eating larger meals will make you feel bloated and will probably cause you to eat more than needed. Pare back the portions, but step up the rate. Six small meals are better than three large ones.

Establish a
daily devotional plan.

"If a man's Bible is coming apart,

it is an indication that

he himself is fairly well

put together."

—James Jennings

PIETY

It would be nice if spirituality came out of a box that we could pull from the freezer and microwave on high for two minutes. But it doesn't. There is no instant piety. Like most things, spiritual growth requires effort.

Your life has individual parts—physical, mental, social, and spiritual. Neglect any of the areas, and imbalance results. Fitness begins on the inside. Make a plan to grow spiritually. Set a daily appointment for prayer and meditation. Allot some time for Scripture and devotional reading. Ask the Lord for strength to meet your goals.

A little boy knocked on a big door in a rather upscale section of town. The butler answered, "May I help you, young man?"

"I'm raising money to buy a new house for my mom," the little boy answered.

"My, my!" the butler responded. "That's going to take a lot of money. Are you sure you can do that all by yourself?"

The little boy answered, "Oh, no sir, my brother's gonna help me when he gets done deliverin' his papers."

You don't have to do it alone.

Eat slowly.

"I don't eat snails.

I prefer fast food."

—Strange de Jim

RHYTHM

I t's called "fast food," but that doesn't mean you have to eat it in a hurry. A meal is not a race. There's no gold medal for being the first to finish your fries. There isn't a Hamburger Hall of Fame. And Mr. Guinness, of the Book of World Records, probably doesn't eat where you eat!

Many people eat too quickly. They chomp the chalupas like their visa is going to expire any minute. Eating too fast is just another symptom signaling that we've pushed the fast-forward button of life and can't find the pause. Our stomachs are usually about two bites behind us. But the fast eating will ensure one thing: Sooner or later, our stomachs will catch up—and overtake us!

Find the rhythm. Slow down. Sit down. Chew your food carefully. Savor it; don't inhale it. Eating at a slower pace has several benefits. First, you'll enjoy the food more. Second, you won't be as likely to overeat. Third, your digestion will likely improve. Eat less and chew more. Eating is important to your health. Take the time to do it right.

Order dressing on the side.

"One should eat to live,

not live to eat."

—Molière

REDUCTION

An obviously overweight man asked the waitress for extra salad dressing for his fried chicken salad. Noticing the look of disdain in her eyes, he said, "Don't worry, Miss; I'm going on a 'skippy' diet tomorrow."

"You mean you're just going to eat peanut butter?"

"Oh, no," the dieter assured her. "I mean I'm just going to skip everything that tastes good."

Dieting takes some "skipping." You don't necessarily have to skip everything that tastes good, but you will have to make careful food selections. Reduce your intake of certain substances—mainly fat. One place to start is by reducing your consumption of salad dressing. Salad dressing is a "sleeper" source of fat; it doesn't seem fatty, but it is. It's deceivingly beautiful, meandering in colorful little rivers over your lettuce. But it can be as ferocious as a tiger, crouching down below the rim of tiny plastic cups, waiting to pounce on your food and turn it into future flab.

Make a healthy choice. Order your dressing on the side. That way you control the amount you consume.

Build on your past successes!

"Life is hard, by the yard;

But by the inch, life's a cinch!"

—Jean L. Gordon

IMPETUS

If you look only at the ultimate goal, you'll likely become discouraged. The end is so far away! Learn to mix short views into your long-range plan. You can accomplish a lot if you take it a little at a time.

Concentrate on reaching some short-range goals. And then use the impetus of reaching those goals as mental fuel to help you reach your longer-range goals. Climb the diet stairs one step at a time. You've added exercise to your life. Great! Now eliminate snacking. You've lost three pounds. Fantastic! You're three pounds closer to your goal. Build on that victory.

A middle-aged woman was huffing and puffing as she did her deep knee bends. "I've almost reached my goal!" she announced excitedly.

"Which one?" her personal trainer asked. "The one where you finally do thirty knee bends a day?"

"No," the lady answered, "the one where my legs have enough muscle to hold up the rest of me!"

You'll never reach your goal by taking one giant step. Take the journey one step (or one knee bend) at a time.

Enjoy a favorite food once in a while.

"Everything you see,

I owe to spaghetti."

—Sophia Loren

ENJOYMENT

It was week number two at the health spa— fourteen days of lettuce, tiny chunks of chicken, three-mile runs, and total dessert abstinence. One of the residents commented to her partner, as they struggled to do their umpteenth sit-up, "Two more days of this stuff, and then I can assure you there'll be some 'pie in the *thigh* by and by!'"

Who says you can't have any fun in life? Just because you're dieting doesn't mean that your life has to be all work and no play. In fact, you may want to plan for some fun. Momentary breaks in the diet routine may be just the thing to keep you on track. It's okay to splurge a little as long as you're under control. Do you like ice cream? Why not have some on your birthday? Do you go wild for a good hot dog? Have one at the ballpark. Keep your intake within the limits you've set for yourself, but don't be afraid to enjoy life.

Choose whole grain breads.

"What we need is a Million-pound
March on Washington
to encourage our legislators
to treat obesity as a major
health problem."

—Samuel Klein

ASSORTMENT

A grocery store clerk was adding up the items on the conveyer belt. The scanner wouldn't register the price on the coffee creamer, so he asked his manager, who was checking out the customer's groceries at the next counter, "What's half-and-half?"

Without looking up, the manager answered, "The last I knew, it was a whole."

Did you ever consider bread as a health food? It could be, if you make the right choice. Walk down the bakery aisle at any supermarket, and you'll be amazed at the choices. You'll see more varieties of bread than there are buttons on a wedding gown!

But not all breads have been *raised* the same way. Some are much better for you than others. And isn't that what dieting is all about: choosing the better? Of course, the better might not be your first choice. "Cinnamon raisin or nothing," you may say. But you might need to choose another lifeline before you give your final answer. Choose whole grain bread. Your whole body will say "Thank you!"

Read all
food labels.

"I am allergic to food. Every time
I eat, it breaks out in fat."

—Jennifer Greene Duncan

AWARENESS

If you saw a piece of apple pie sitting on a trash can in the park, you wouldn't dream of putting it in your mouth. Just because it's food doesn't mean it's good for you. So don't assume that everything on the store shelf is good for you. It may be sanitary but still not what your body needs. Be aware of what you allow to pass over your lips.

A teenager rushed from the kitchen into the family room where Grandma, who was visiting in the home, sat in the lounge chair reading her Bible. "Whatcha doing, Gramma," the teen said flippantly, "studyin' for your finals?"

Studying can really pay off, even when picking out food. Food product labels make for some interesting reading. Study them carefully. What's good for you? What should you avoid? It's all there in black and white. Think before you eat. It'll be good for you in the end.

Invest in a
low-fat cookbook.

"The two biggest sellers in my
bookstore are the cookbooks
and the diet books. The cookbooks
tell you how to prepare the food
and the diet books tell you
how not to eat any of it."

—Andy Rooney

TECHNIQUE

A husband came home from the mall bookstore with a book titled *Seven Daily Menus under Two Thousand Calories*. Handing it to his wife, he said, "I bought something for our future, dear."

She took the book from him, gave him a kiss on the cheek, and said, "Thanks, honey! That'll help us get rid of what's behind us too!"

Deciding to eat properly is one thing. Knowing how to prepare nutritious meals is something else. Learn how to cook low-fat meals. That will mean knowing *which foods* to prepare, as well as knowing *how* to prepare them.

The first step is to buy a good cookbook. If you can't find one on the rows of books at the corner book mart, you may find one on the Internet. Be selective. Find one that will support the direction your diet is taking, not just one that has a pretty picture on the cover. Then spend some time learning to cook a new way. It will help with what's ahead of you and what's behind you.

Replace
sweets with fruits.

"Avoid fruits and nuts.

You are what you eat."

—Garfield

ALTERNATIVES

U pon arriving at the Hershey chocolate plant, the wife of one of my friends opened the car door and commented, "This must be what Heaven smells like."

We've become a society that marks its events not only with cards and ceremonies but also with the purchase of chocolate. And, for some, a historic event isn't even necessary! Our love for chocolate is nothing to *snicker* about. Sure, it tastes good. But is it good for us? Chocolate contains caffeine, and it's high in sugar. To some, it's an issue as important as morning coffee and afternoon Oprah: They can't get through the day without either one.

But there's more than one way to satisfy your craving for sweets. Part of the thrill of dieting is in the discovery of alternative foods. Fruit is a good alternative. It's sweet to the taste and much better for you. Peel a banana. Slice some oranges. Dip an apple. Pop a grape. Do what you have to in order to avoid the "gold in them thar Hershey plants."

Check with the doctor at the halfway point.

"Doctors tell us there are over seventeen million people who are overweight. These, of course, are only round figures."

—Jay Leno

COUNSEL

A wife dialed 911 in a panic, "My husband is turning blue! What should I do?"

The naive new operator replied, "Have you tried singing cheerful songs?"

Most medical advice is far better than that. And you should seek it along the way. Dieting represents significant change in your life. Are those changes really good for you? Diet books call for exercise. But is your body up to that? You've cut back on your food intake. But are you eating the right things?

Reading the "expert advice" on the covers of those magazines in the grocery checkout lane isn't exactly the best way to approach health care. And watching a documentary about emergency rooms on cable television doesn't exactly make you a medical expert. You need some outside advice. Keep in touch with your physician throughout your weight-loss program. Not only will your physician start you down the diet road, but he or she will also set up a checkpoint along the way. And a halfway checkup is a good idea.

Save your snack money and buy some new clothes!

"A person who is overweight
is living beyond his seams."

—Steve Weber

COMPENSATION

"Congratulations!" the exercise coach said to her trainee. "You just completed that ten-minute exercise in less than thirty minutes!"

Learn to congratulate yourself. How about giving yourself some dieters' compensation. If workers' compensation is a law in industry, then dieters' compensation should be a law in dieting. You've suffered through the loss of mashed potatoes and gravy. Now it's time for the reward.

"You deserve a break today," the commercial advises. That break doesn't have to be down at the Baskin-Robbins ice cream store. And you may be too tired (or too weak) to pat yourself on the back. But you can treat yourself. Just make sure that treat is something other than food. If you're doing well on your resolves, find a way to compensate yourself. You might buy some new clothes with the money you've saved by eating right. Or you might indulge yourself with a good book or a weekend getaway. Don't make your diet drudgery. Give yourself something to work toward. Set some short-term goals. When you reach them, celebrate!

Value the
gift of life.

"If you have good eyesight
and good hearing, thank God who
gave them to you."

—Proverbs 20:12

THANKSGIVING

I t used to be that the only place you would say "Take a little off the top" was in the corner barbershop. Now it's a popular saying in the plastic surgeon's office as well—along with "Take a little off the bottom" and "Take a little off the sides." Packaging isn't just a problem in manufacturing anymore. It has invaded our culture and has affected the way we look at ourselves. But the most important thing about us isn't skin, muscle, or bone. *Who* we are is far more important than what we look like.

You have a lot going for you, even if there are things about your life that you'd like to change—and there must be, or you wouldn't be reading this book! But there are probably more things for which you can be thankful. Make a list. Name the things that you like about *you*. Get in the habit of counting your blessings, along with counting your calories. Begin with the blessing of life.

No matter what happens, keep trying.

"Paralyze resistance
with persistence."

—Woody Hayes

RESOLVE

There are some days when it just doesn't pay to go to work. That's probably what the bank robber thought when he wrote his holdup note on his bank deposit slip—and then left it on the bank counter.

There will be days when you are tempted to quit your diet. You're on a journey, and you can be sure there will be a few construction zones along the way. At times you'll agree with that sign held by the flagman: "Slow Construction." You'll even be tempted to take the next exit ramp. You'll face setbacks. You'll *add* and *multiply* some pounds instead of *subtracting*.

Maybe you're at that point right now. But don't quit! Resolve to reach your goal in spite of setbacks. Every achievement, from the invention of the lightbulb to the walk on the moon, has had its momentary defeats. But someone refused to accept a defeat as final. Never give in to the notion that you can't win. Resolve to reach your goal. You will be a healthier, happier person. Keep going. You will win!

Never fear failure.

"Failure isn't bitter if you

don't swallow it."

—Chris Rock

CONFIDENCE

T he only thing we have to fear is fear itself," former president Franklin D. Roosevelt proclaimed. But he probably hadn't been in the passenger side of the car when that teenager took her first solo drive! Fear keeps you alert, but it doesn't have to keep you in chains. You may hit a pothole on the road to your weight-loss goals, but that doesn't mean you have to wreck your diet. It just means you'll need an alignment. You don't have to be listed as a casualty. Failure isn't fatal; the fear of it is. Fear is paralyzing. It locks you in place. It prevents you from trying, let alone succeeding.

Don't be afraid to fail. In fact, you should count on it. There's no chance that you'll *never* fail in life. That doesn't mean you'll never reach your goal. It simply means that you'll take a couple of steps backward once in a while. So what? Your failures don't own you. You own them. And as you learn from them, they'll become weaker, and you'll become stronger.

Be patient with yourself.

"The second day of a diet is

always easier than the first.

By the second day you're off it."

—Jackie Gleason

PATIENCE

A lady concerned about her friend's overweight condition invited her to go horseback riding for some exercise. Reluctantly the friend agreed and, with some effort, finally slithered and squirmed into an old pair of jeans. With a little help, she also put on a pair of cowboy boots. After the whole dressing ordeal, the friend said to the new cowgirl, "You look great!"

"I don't feel so great," she answered.

"Why's that?" her friend inquired.

"I was just thinking about that horse. He thinks he's going jogging, but it'll be more like weight lifting."

You may be your own worst critic. Nobody knows your faults better than you do, and nobody has a greater stake in the success of your resolve. That makes a powerful motive for being hard on yourself. Be patient. Give yourself some time to make changes. Understand that you won't do it right the first time. Cut yourself some slack, and don't become frustrated with slow progress. Just be sure you're on the right path.

Think: "Today
is a brand-new start!"

"Don't let yesterday use up

too much of today."

—Will Rogers

OPTIMISM

Surprised to see the words "Shake and Bake" on his wife's refrigerator-door calendar, a husband asked, "What's this?"

"It's simple," his wife replied. "On Tuesdays I go to my aerobics class the first thing in the morning, and then I stop off at the tanning salon on the way home!"

There is a bright side to every day, and it starts first thing in the morning. Every day, you have the opportunity to wipe the slate clean and start over. Yesterday's triumphs and traumas are history. Today's opportunities are as fresh as the sunrise. Every day brings a new chance to succeed.

Maybe you fell off the diet wagon yesterday. That double-dark fudge cake was just too inviting. "Why did I do that?" you ask. It's simple: Your "want to" got the best of the situation! But today's another day. It's time to begin again. Today, you can become smarter, stronger, and more able. Plant that thought in your mind. Today is the day that you have to work with. Make the most of it.

Stay on track!

"You can tell when you are on the right road—it's all uphill."

—Joyce Meyer

SINGLE-MINDEDNESS

Signing up at the local health club for the third time, a lady asked the front-desk attendant what category she should mark on the application. Knowing the lady's history of joining and then forsaking her membership commitments, she replied, "Temporary help."

Successful dieting is not a once-in-a-while convenience. It is a long-term commitment, a commitment that must not be swayed by distractions. There are many things that may distract you from your weight-loss goal, but food is the least of them. You may become content, thinking that your progress to date is good enough. Or you may take on a new interest or hobby, robbing energy that you need for exercise. You may even become busy at work and slide back into poor eating habits as a way of saving time.

Don't lose your focus like a cross-eyed javelin thrower. You need a clear vision of the target. You need to stay focused on your diet goals and refuse to give time or energy to distractions. Be single-minded. Keep your eyes on the road.

Ask God for special strength when tempted.

"Unless there is within us
that which is above us,
we will soon yield to that
which is around us."

—C. Hastings Smith

PRAYER

You have a resource available to you that many people don't know about and fewer take advantage of. It's called prayer. When you face the temptation to break your resolves, to slip back into unhealthy habits and attitudes, ask God for strength.

You may have a diet partner, but there will still be those times you feel so very alone. For example, you may be the only person at the restaurant table who doesn't order a dessert. Or you may have your own food at the family dinner table. While everyone else at the table is ladling gravy on their mashed potatoes, you're using low-fat margarine.

Don't forget: You are not alone in your struggle. The God who created you really does care about you— every inch of you (including the extra inches).

Thanks to modern technology, we can pick up the phone (even in the automobile) and access the counsel and comfort of friends, associates, or counselors. But the greatest opportunity is even more convenient. God's counsel is as close as a prayer.

Be disciplined.

"One way to get rid of weight

is to leave it on the plate."

—Chuck Millhuff

RESTRAINT

A little girl came running into the house crying. "What's wrong, honey?" her mother asked.

Between sobs and sniffs, the little girl said, "Candy, the girl down the street, has a bunch of cool Barbie doll clothes, and I traded her a kitten from Tabby's litter for some of them. And now I want some more!"

Trying to console her little girl, her mom asked, "Is she all out of clothes?"

"No, Mom," she answered.

"Well, what's the problem then?" Mom asked.

The little girl sobbed, "I'm all out of kittens!"

Too much dieting is as bad as too little. When the whole weight-loss process begins to take its toll on our physical, financial, social, and spiritual lives, it may be time to show a little restraint. Restraint means "to bring under control." To restrain yourself, to discipline yourself, is to take control of yourself. It means making decisions with your mind, rather than your appetite. It means being the master of your own life.

Keep a journal.

"It's not a bad idea to get in
the habit of writing down one's
thoughts. It saves one having to
bother anyone else with them."

—Isabel Colegate

OBSERVATION

"I just discovered a fantastic new way to remember my wedding anniversary," Fred exclaimed to his tennis partner.

"Tell me!" his partner said excitedly.

"I forgot it," Fred answered.

"You mean you forgot the new way to remember your anniversary?"

Fred replied, "No. I mean my anniversary was today, and I forgot it!"

It's amazing what a little note taking will do for you—including the remembrance of your anniversary. The keeping of a personal journal has been revived in these days. Bookstores and greeting-card shops have done a brisk business in selling hardbound books filled with empty pages. Those pages are then filled with the reflections of the journal writer—reflections of joys and sorrows, losses and gains. In fact, looking back can be just as valuable as looking ahead. What happened today? Why? What does it mean?

Journaling is a valuable tool for observing your diet program. Use it to keep in touch with yourself, pondering the things that have been in order to take control of the things that will be.

Hire a
personal trainer.

"As a coach, I have to make
the players do what they don't
want to do in order to achieve
what they want to achieve."

—Bob Stoops

TRAINING

Are you sure that new trainer has always worked in the physical-fitness industry?" the concerned health-club member asked the club manager.

He replied, "Madam, that trainer was recommended by my best friend. I'm sure her credentials are impeccable."

The lady responded, "Well, I thought you might like to know that at the end of my workout today, she put a blanket over me and led me around the gym!"

Exercising on your own is good, as far as it goes. But you may get more benefit from your effort if you exercise under the direction of a trainer. Of course, you'll want to know what the credentials of that trainer really are! But a personal trainer can personalize your exercise program and offer valuable advice toward reaching your exercise goals.

What heart rate should you maintain during exercise? How long should you exercise during each session? What forms of exercise will complement your aerobic workout? Many people don't know how to evaluate these questions. A personal trainer can help.

**Read good
books on effective
dieting.**

"Reading is to the mind
what exercise is to the body."

—Joseph Addison

INQUIRY

Two friends were going through the diet-book section of the bookstore. One commented, "You know, I just don't understand why they have cookbooks on one shelf and diet books right next to them."

Her friend answered, "It's probably so you'll have a better idea of what you shouldn't eat!"

Get your mind involved in the war on weight. Willpower alone will not achieve your weight-loss goal. You want to do more than shed pounds. You want to change your habits to improve your overall health. To do that, you will need to gather some outside resources. From the book-of-the-month club to the Internet, there are probably more diet helps available than ever before. But collecting books on dieting and neglecting to read them is like getting on an exercise bike and never peddling.

Study the subject of diet and nutrition. Read everything you can on the subject of health. Avoid sensational reading that promises quick results. Dig into the subject. Challenge yourself to learn. Just as a waist can be a terrible thing to mind, a mind is a terrible thing to waste.

Stretch before breakfast.

"Another good reducing
exercise consists in placing
both hands against the table
edge and pushing back."

—Robert Quillen

FLEXIBILITY

Taking a picture of a Buckingham Palace guard marching slowly and stoically in front of a guardhouse, a visitor to London commented to her husband, "Oh, look, dear. He looks like you when you get up in the morning to start the coffee!"

As we age, our muscles not only move around our bodies, they develop an attitude. They get stubborn. It's as if they say to our mind, "You go on ahead, I'll join you later."

That's why we should strive to stay flexible.

Stretching is one way to maintain that flexibility. Obviously, stretching is good for your health. People wear *stretch* pants. Horses gallop down the home *stretch*. We *stretch* our budgets and *stretch* our time. Why, even major-league baseball comes to a halt in the seventh inning for a corporate flexing.

Start your day with a *stretch* instead of *starch*; it'll get your blood moving and make you feel more alert. When your muscles are strong and supple, you'll feel better. And, while you're at it, give your mind a morning stretch as well.

Purchase a treadmill.

"The person who does not
find time for exercise may
have to find time for illness."

—Dr. Tim Johnson

EXERCISE

People's exercise regimens run the gamut from a daily one-mile jog to an eighteen-inch bend to pick up the morning paper. One of the benefits of exercise is its routine. Disciplined exercise leads to disciplined dieting.

You don't have to run a footrace with that neighbor's Doberman to obtain the benefits of exercise; you can stay in the house. One hotel chain even offers exercise equipment as a room service. It will probably never take the place of a seven-dollar bagel and a cold cup of coffee, but at least it's an alternative.

The sun can take a break from shining, but you need to stick with your routine rain or shine. If your only option for exercise is outdoors, you may miss too many opportunities. One answer is to buy a treadmill. Walking is one of the best forms of exercise, and if you can do it indoors, you'll have no excuse to avoid working out. You can even double-time on the treadmill by listening to the radio, watching television, or even reading.

Combine exercise and fellowship: Take a walk with a friend.

"My best friend is the one who brings out the best in me."

—Henry Ford

COMPANIONSHIP

Misery loves company," the saying goes. It's either a good commentary on life or a description of walking with a friend on a hot August day, trying to fit into last November's jogging suit! Even the dulling routine of daily exercise is made a little more palatable if you have an exercise partner. Companionship is one of our basic needs. Why should we abandon it when we go on a diet? In fact, companionship can be a great incentive to dieting.

"Am I still your Dreamboat?" a wife asked her husband on their twenty-fifth anniversary.

"Absolutely, dear," he answered. "But I guess we both need a little more dock space than we used to!"

If you're having trouble reaching your diet goals, get some help. Find a buddy to walk with. You'll reach two goals at once: relationship building and fitness. Far from being a dreaded discipline, your daily walk will become a treasured appointment. It will become your time to unwind, unload, listen, and talk. It'll strengthen your heart in two ways.

Join a
health club.

"Joined a health club last year,

spent four hundred bucks.

Haven't lost a pound. Apparently,

you have to show up."

—Rich Ceisler

REGIMEN

I heard of a memory expert who had to cancel a lecture because, when he got to the auditorium, he realized he had forgotten his notes. Everybody, including the experts, needs a little lift once in a while. When all the dieting home remedies fail, it may be time to get some help. Maybe it's time to rejuvenate that rice-and-carrot-dandruff diet with a regimen of focused exercise. Maybe it's time to join the neighborhood health club. It may cost you a membership fee, but think of it as a good investment—considering hospital costs these days. When you've paid for something, you take it seriously. And the fact that you've paid for the privilege of working your body may make you more likely to do it.

You'll also find a wider assortment of exercise options. Free weights, stair machines, station-ery bicycles, and even a swimming pool may be available to you instead of that same old walk around the block.

Resolve to
stay youthful.

"The secret to staying young
is to live honestly, eat slowly,
and lie about your age."

—Lucille Ball

VIEWPOINT

Dealing with her two unruly grand-children, Grandma commented, "You can't pull the wool over my eyes, young men. I was your age too!"

One of the boys nudged the other and whispered, "Must be the long-term memory that's the last to go!"

Age isn't a number. It's a viewpoint. Think young, and you'll be healthier. If you visualize yourself as getting old, you're probably old (or soon will be). Conversely, if you think of yourself as young, your body may be playing taps, but your mind will be playing reveille.

There are many ways you can spend your day. You can choose the *safe* or you can choose the *spectacular*. You can crack walnuts under your rocking chair, or you can go scooter surfing. Go for the scooter ride! Try new things. Make a point of mixing with younger people. Keep an open mind. Stay out late once in a while. You really are as young as you feel, at least in terms of your attitude. Keep your viewpoint young, and your body will feel younger too.

Find motivation in someone who's done it!

"Learn from the skillful;

he who teaches himself has

a fool for a master."

—Chinese Proverb

EXAMPLE

After a tumultuous discussion over the grocery bill, the newlywed wife exclaimed to her husband, "I just hate it when you get so historical!"

Not wanting to add more fuel to the fire, he said rather softly, "I believe you meant to say 'hysterical,' not 'historical.'"

"I know exactly what I meant to say!" his wife shot back. "I hate it when you get historical! I hate it when you drag up the past!"

There are those who would douse your diet flame with *unholy water*. But even as they criticize your past efforts, they are probably envying your courage. Why listen to the critics when you can set your sights on an example of the very thing you desire to be? Many have been where you are. Losing weight and improving health are not superhuman goals. Lots of real people have accomplished this, probably even someone you know. Find one of those people, and learn from him or her. Find out how they handled setbacks and failures. Learn their success story. Let it inspire you to write one of your own.

Feed your soul daily!

"Feed your faith, and your doubts will starve to death."

—Billy Graham

SPIRITUALITY

U pset that his junior-high son was spending too much time in front of the computer screen, Dad commented, "Son, all you do is fool around with that computer! You're neglecting more important things!"

The boy suddenly stopped and turned to his father, "Like what, Dad?"

The father replied, "Well, like religious things. Why, I bet you don't even know where to find the Sermon on the Mount!"

"That's simple!" the son responded, as he turned back to the computer. "I'll just run a search!"

If you improve only your physical health, you've reached only half the goal. You need spiritual health just as much as physical. That, too, requires good nutrition. Don't neglect your soul. Feed it good things every day. Have a helping of encouragement. Load your plate with love. Sip on some scripture. Take liberal doses of meditation and prayer. If your life is to be in balance, your spirit must be well-nourished. You're very concerned about the part of you that everyone sees. Don't neglect the part that only God sees.

About the Author

An international speaker, best-selling author and compassionate teacher, Stan has authored more than 90 books to date. Best sellers include *The Secret Blend; God Has Never Failed Me, but He's Sure Scared Me to Death a Few Times; The Buzzards Are Circling, but God's Not Finished with Me Yet; ReThink Your Life;* his popular Minute Motivators series; and his newest book,  *TERRIFIC! Five Star Customer Service.* His books have sold more than three million copies worldwide.

Stan served for 40 years as a pastor, and was named general superintendent emeritus by the Church of the Nazarene denomination. In addition to his writing, he was vice president of John Maxwell's Injoy Ministries, has spoken in 80 countries, and shared the platform with speakers including Zig Ziglar, Jerry Lucas, Rick Warren, Bill Hybels, and Cy Young Award winner R. A. Dickey.

To Contact the Author
Visit www.stantoler.com.